Caleb

and

The Trash Fairy

The Trash Fairy
Caleb and the box car race

Written & illustrated
by Jenene Snyder
2014

I dedicate this book to my Grandson Caleb Jack Perry.
I love you very much. May God bless you as you grow.
May your life be filled with kindness, love and peace.

A special thanks to, Charlie Smith and Pat Richmond.
Without their support this book would not exist.

A special thanks to, little Jaycee May McKeithen.

Caleb was a happy, busy little boy, who was always making messes. Like most little boys he hated cleaning up after himself. Caleb's parents scolded him often about cleaning up his room and picking up his trash. Caleb just didn't think it was that important. His dad and mom would say to him, "Do you think the Trash fairy lives here? Messes don't just clean themselves. Life is a lot easier when things are kept clean and organized."

This year Caleb had turned 9 years old, and old enough to enter the Boxcar Derby race. The rules say, the children could help each other on their cars; however, the majority of the project had to be completed by the contestants. Caleb's father could help, by letting him use tools for the project and offering some advice, of course.

Collecting Items for the box car

Caleb spent the entire week collecting a wooden crate from the local Market; wheels from an old bike, a rod for the steering wheel and lots of other items build his Boxcar out of. He found bits and pieces, from things the neighbors had left on the curb, for the Trash Man. All week he had collected the parts, until he finally had almost enough parts for his Boxcar.

Saturday came and Caleb had two weeks to put the Boxcar together and to do the practice runs with, before the race. He really wanted to win, so it would take a lot of practice. Caleb didn't even finish his breakfast, before running out to the garage to get started.

But, oh boy, when he got to the garage, it was a huge mess. Caleb's dad had told him last week to clean out the garage, before he started to collect the items for the Boxcar. Caleb hardly knew where to start. His friend Jack brought some pedals, paint, lumber and things, from when he and his dad cleaned, their garage out. This added to the clutter.

Gathering the frame, Caleb mounted the wheels on the axle. While he was working, Jack showed up to help. Then Caleb added the body, then the seat that he made from the wooden crate. Fishing through the rubble wasn't easy, but Caleb and Jack put each piece together until the Boxcar was almost finished.

Caleb's dad entered the garage and told Caleb to clean up the mess and put the tools away, when he finished. The two boys worked all day on the Boxcar, "I'll clean up the mess tomorrow." Caleb told Jack. "I am too tired to do it today." I wish the Trash Fairy did live here, and then she could clean the garage, Caleb thought.

By the next week Caleb had finished his Boxcar and was ready to try it out. He and Jack pushed it to the race track, for a test run. For two blocks they pushed and pulled. They couldn't figure out why his Boxcar would not roll easily. By the time they got to the track they were very tired. Jack stated, "It will roll easily as soon as we place it the car on the hill."

Finally, they got the Boxcar to the top of the hill, and Caleb climbed into the seat. Caleb hollered to Jack, "Pull the blocks out from under the wheels." Jack did, but the Boxcar would not roll very fast. Disappointed and tired, the boys dragged the Boxcar back home.

At the dinner table Caleb's dad and mom asked about his Boxcar. Caleb told them about his problem. "Did you grease the wheels?" His dad asked. "That's what I forgot" Caleb replied.

Now he knew what to do. The next day Caleb was searching for the grease gun to fix the wheels. He looked and looked but he could not find it.

When Caleb asked his dad, if he knew where the grease gun was.   His dad told him, "If you had straightened up the garage, before you built the Boxcar, then you would be able to find things, when you need them. Sadly, Caleb said, "I forgot." His dad replied, "Remember the Trash Fairy doesn't live here." Then Dad told Caleb to go out after lunch and clean the garage.

As Caleb was cleaning, he found the grease gun. He was really excited and immediately greased the wheels on the Boxcar. He called Jack, and again they took the Boxcar to the race track for another test run. This time the Boxcar rolled easily. When they got to the top of the hill, Caleb told Jack, "Pull out the blocks!" When Jack did the Boxcar started rolling faster and faster, "Like greeease lightnin!" Caleb shouted. The boys were so excited. Caleb knew he could win the race, and now his dream would come true.

Each day as Caleb worked; the mess in the garage seemed twice as large as the day before. Caleb would ask his parents if they knew where this is, or that is, never being able to find anything in all the clutter and trash.

His dad would say, "If you would clean up your mess and throw away your trash, at the end of the day, you would be able to find, what you want, when you need it." Being organized and neat makes life a whole lot easier. Being able to find things without searching is a blessing.

Caleb worked daily on his Boxcar. He painted it fire engine red, with flames on the sides and put his assigned number seven, on the hood, on the front of the Boxcar. He painted the seat dark blue. For the windshield he used a piece of Plexiglas the he had found in the trash. It looked as good as any Boxcar ever looked. The best one ever! Caleb thought.

The day of the race

Finally the day of the big race came. Caleb and Jack got the Boxcar out of the garage and started adding the final touches. Caleb said to Jack, "Will you get the grease gun out of the garage?" Jack went into the garage and stood in the middle of a huge mess. He looked and looked but he could not find the grease gun.

Jack ran out and told Caleb that he couldn't find the grease gun in all that clutter. Caleb went into the garage; he couldn't believe how messy the garage was. It looked like a disastrous storm had struck the whole garage. Tools were mixed in with trash and spare parts. He too could not find the grease gun.

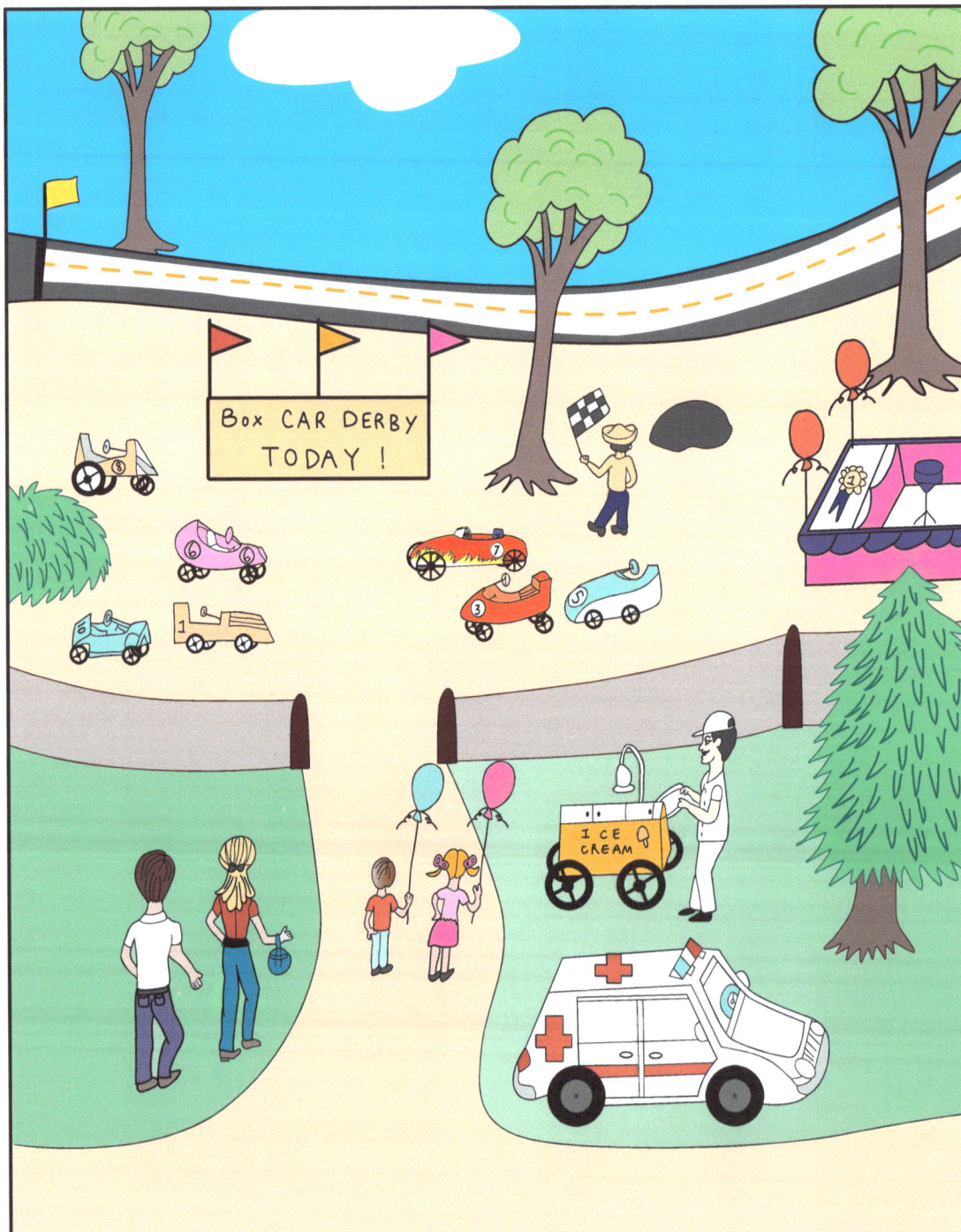

Finally, Caleb decided the Boxcar would race just fine without more grease. They had to leave now or they would be late for the race.

As Caleb and Jack arrived at the park, they were so excited to see all the different Boxcars. They were all kinds of shapes, sizes and colors. Caleb went to the entry booth and got his position for the race.

Caleb's heart was pounding with joy as he and Jack pushed the Boxcar to the starting line. Caleb took his position and climbed in his Boxcar. Then a Judge told the boys, "As soon as you hear the whistle, have your assistants pull the blocks out from under the wheels." Suddenly the whistle blew. The blocks were pulled and the Boxcars started to roll down the hill. Faster and faster the Boxcars went

as they zoomed past the bystanders. Caleb was out in front. Then, suddenly, his Boxcar started slowing down, slower and slower, until it came to a stop.

He heard a Judge announce the winner. If only he had found the grease gun. The wheels had stuck and would no longer turn.

Dad and Mom helped Caleb load the Boxcar onto the truck and take it home. All the way home, the ride was quiet. Caleb did have fun and that was the most important part of any contest.   However, he was still sad he didn't win.

When they arrived at home, Caleb's dad said, "I am sorry you didn't win Son, but this should teach you something you will always remember. If you had cleaned up the garage, thrown away the trash, organized and put things where they belonged, you would have been able to find the grease gun."

He knew his father was right. The very next day he cleaned up the garage and he found the grease gun. Caleb was sad, but now he kne how important it is to keep things clean, tidy and free of trash.

Caleb also decided to clean his room. Caleb found the baseball glove that he had been looking for. "Wow, this is a blessing to find things without all the clutter," he thought.

Caleb took out a poster, sat down at his desk and started to draw a picture. Then his dad entered the room and he was completely surprised at how clean Caleb's room was. "Well, Son, I am sorry you lost the race but, there is always next year. I am sure you will win it then. It looks like you have learned from this. You and your room look so clean and neat." His dad said.

Caleb said, "I know now how important it is to keep things clean and tidy. If I had, I would have found the grease gun, and I would have won the race." His dad noticed Caleb writing something on a poster, he walked over to him and asked, "What is that you're writing on?" Caleb told him, "I'll show you." Caleb walked over to the wall and hung his poster on it.

It was the Trash Fairy is sitting on top of the trash can filing her nails. Caleb wrote these words on the poster, it said:

The Trash Fairy History

The Trash Fairy came about in a funny way, a few decades. ago...

Here is how it all began. Each morning when I left for work our house would be clean. In the evenings when i returned, it looked like a tornado had struck it. I would leave a coffee cup, bowl and spoon in the sink and return to messes everywhere. There would be crumbs, dirty dishes, liquid spills, and trash all over the kitchen. Coats and shoes were everywhere and the living room had clutter from items not being returned to their proper places. The kid's room was always a disaster and the trash was over flowing from not being emptied... when it was more than obvious to ANYONE that it needed to be taken out. Frustrated, I would do as most women do and complain and comment about the messes. However, it never seemed to fix the issue. It all seemed hopeless!

One morning after rising and walking to the kitchen to pour a cup of coffee I thought to myself... 'I just don't think that I can stand coming home to a messy house anymore.' I made a plan to have a talk with my family that night.

After dinner, I announced that we all needed to go into the living room and have a family conference. I explained that I don't get to do the things I want, when I want, no one does. Yet, everyone here only thinks about what they want for themselves and that is selfish. "just think of the fun we could have as a family if I didn't have to spend so much time making sure everyone picks up after themselves. Think of how nice it would be if I had a smile on my face rather than a frown and grouchy voice. No one wants to hear anybody complain all of the time." I made it clear to all that from now on I was not going to cook if I had to come home and be the nagging housekeeper. That in itself is a full time job! We were a team and family members help each other. That is what family is all about. Do your chores and clean up after yourselves.

As I spoke, I got more and more frustrated as though no one would listen. Then i got louder and said, "What do you think I am, The Trash Fairy or something? Poof! I swing my wand and the dishes are done. Poof! I swing my wand and the coats are hung. Poof! I swing my wand and the trash jumps into the trash can?"

The next evening as I left work, I dreaded going home as I knew the house would be a mess. When I arrived, the kitchen was a mess. My heart sunk! I would wait till everyone got home and I would make them clean up the kitchen. Reaching for a glass to get a drink of water, I moved the cereal box to the side and low and behold... there was a quarter under it. I laughed out loud. I picked up the bowl next to it and there was a dime under it. As I walked around the kitchen cleaning and laughing, I collected the change.

I knew our little talk was successful Finally my family knew that it was important to do their chores and help out around the house. It frees my time so that our family can enjoy more fun things to do together. Now, I do walk about with a smile on my face!

Can you draw a picture of a Trash Can here?

www.ingramcontent.com/pod-product-compliance
Lightning Source LLC
Chambersburg PA
CBHW042113040426
42448CB00002B/253